J
552
Gal

JUL 2001

Gallant, Roy A.

Rocks

DUE DATE

6/04 x 9			
8/04 11			

KALEIDOSCOPE

ROCKS

by

Roy A. Gallant

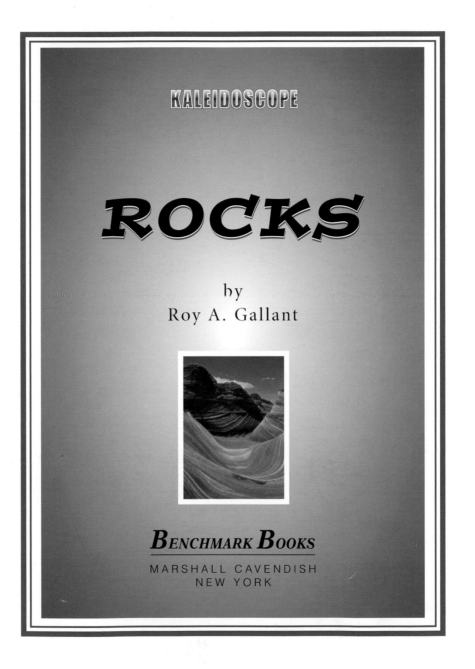

BENCHMARK BOOKS

MARSHALL CAVENDISH
NEW YORK

Series consultant:
Dr. Jerry LaSala, Chariman
Department of Physics
University of Southern Maine

Benchmark Books
Marshall Cavendish Corporation
99 White Plains Road
Tarrytown, NY 10591

Library of Congress Cataloging-in-Publication Data

Gallant, Roy A.
Rocks / by Roy A. Gallant
p.cm.
Includes bibliographical references and index.
Summary: Describes the three types of rocks and how each type is formed and becomes part of the rock cycle.
ISBN 0-7614-1042-2
1. Rocks—Juvenile literature. [1. Rocks] I. Title. II. Kaledioscope (Tarrytown, N.Y.)
QE432.2.G28   2000   552—dc2199-047493

Photo research by Candlepants, Inc.
Cover photo © Photo Researchers
Photo credits: Photo Researchers: cover, 5, 6, 9, 10, 13, 14, 19, 20, 23, 24, 27, 28-29, 31, 32, 35, 39, 40, 43. Earth Scenes: 15, 16.
Diagram on page 37 by Gysela Pacheco.

Printed in Italy.

6 5 4 3 2 1

CONTENTS

ABOUT ROCKS

The next time you go on a hike, take a good look around. You will see many different kinds of rocks —from tiny pebbles to huge boulders. Grab a fistful of rocks. What color are they? Are they a mixture of colors? Some may have been worn and are smooth to touch. Others may have been broken and have sharp, jagged edges. A mountain is a huge lump of rock that is millions of years old.

Round and smooth rocks like these have been worn smooth by thousands of years of tumbling by water.

Planet Earth is a giant rock. So is the Moon. In most places the solid rock ground, or *bedrock*, is covered by soil, plants, and oceans. But sometimes it is exposed. Rocks are everywhere. But they don't grow the way plants or animals do. Have you ever wondered where rocks come from?

Rock layers millions of years old are revealed wherever road cuts, such as this one in Maryland, expose the bedrock.

ANIMAL, VEGETABLE, OR MINERAL?

Rocks are made of different kinds of *minerals* packed together. A mineral is a natural, nonliving substance found in the ground. Some minerals are very hard, such as diamonds. Others may be soft and crumbly, like talc. A mineral always looks and feels the same no matter where in the world you find it. Great pressure deep inside Earth squeezes and cements different minerals together, turning them into rocks.

Minerals are the building blocks of rocks. This polished mineral crystal is muscovite, useful as an electrical insulator.

Granite is a kind of rock made of the minerals quartz, mica, and feldspar. If you look closely at a chunk of granite, you will see bits of milky quartz, smooth black mica, and reddish feldspar. Unlike minerals, rocks may vary from place to place, depending on the amounts of each mineral present. If there is more feldspar than mica in a piece of granite, for example, the rock may appear reddish instead of gray.

The common rock granite is made up of white quartz crystals, feldspar, and black flakes of mica, all minerals.

HOW ROCKS ARE MADE

Let's look at how Earth turns minerals into rocks. Any rock you ever find will belong to one of three basic types. Each type is made in a certain way.

IGNEOUS (*IG-nee-us*) rock comes from *magma*. Its name means "fire" rock. Deep inside our planet the rock is heated by the great weight of all the rock above pressing down. The rock is heated so much that it melts and becomes the liquid rock we call magma. The magma is then pushed this way and that, like toothpaste when you squeeze the tube. Sometimes it is pushed up through cracks in the bedrock and spreads over the ocean floor. Other times it explodes from the ground as lava from a volcano. More often, though, magma rises only to Earth's crust where it cools.

Hot liquid rock called magma flows out of volcanoes. It then cools and hardens as lava rock, like this flow from Kilauea Volcano in Hawaii.

13

As magma cools, it forms crystals and becomes igneous rock. Sometimes magma cools so quickly that crystals do not form, and the lava turns into volcanic glass, called *obsidian*. Obsidian is usually black, but may also be red or brown. It has edges sharp enough to cut a steak.

When magma cools less rapidly, very small crystal grains form, and the rock is called *basalt*. Most basalt is smooth and dark. When magma cools slowly below Earth's surface, it forms large grains and becomes the igneous rock granite.

SEDIMENTARY (*sed-uh-MEN-tuh-ree*) rock is made when sediments get pressed together deep inside Earth. Sediments might be mud, clay, sand, or gravel. Year after year rivers and streams wash sediments into the oceans. Currents then carry the sediments far out onto the seafloor. Over thousands of years the sediments pile up and form a carpet thicker than the tallest skyscraper. Then something interesting happens.

Soil, clay, and other sediments washed along by a river eventually get deposited at the river's mouth as a delta, such as the Mississippi River Delta.

17

The great weight of the sediments at the top of the pile squeezes the bits and pieces of the deeper sediments tightly together. At the same time, certain chemicals in the water act as a glue that cements the bits and pieces into a solid mass. The mud, clay, sand, or gravel has been turned into sedimentary rock.

Soft sediments flow out onto the sea floor where they are deposited in layers. Eventually, they are compressed as rock. Later, the old seafloor may be thrust up as dry land and reveal the sedimentary rock layering.

19

Thousands or millions of years later, the old sea may slowly dry up and expose the sedimentary rocks as land. Or forces deep within the planet may push the ocean bottom up so that it is left high and dry. This happened to the Alps, the highest mountains in Europe. Long ago they were completely underwater. To this day, you can find fossils of ancient sea creatures among the rocks there—15,000 feet (4,572 meters) above sea level.

Europe's famous mountain, the Matterhorn, is part of the Alps mountain chain and was once buried deep within the seafloor.

If the old sediments happened to be sand, the sedimentary rock is called *sandstone*. It is often tan and feels like sandpaper. If the sediments were mud and silt, the sedimentary rock is called *shale*. Shale is greenish gray and can be split apart in thin layers. Shale makes up more than half of all sedimentary rocks and often contains fossils.

This lovely marcasite "star," made of iron and sulfur, is part of the shale formation of dark rock.

23

A sedimentary rock type called *conglomerate* is formed when the sediments are a mixture of pebbles and small rocks. A piece of conglomerate looks something like a sticky popcorn ball. Still another kind of sedimentary rock is *limestone*.

Limestone is formed when the skeletons of tiny sea animals drift down onto the seafloor and form a sediment carpet that turns into soft, smooth, usually white rock.

England's famous White Cliffs of Dover are made of the sedimentary rock limestone—the compressed skeletons of tiny sea creatures.

METAMORPHIC (*meta-MOR-fick*) rock is formed when igneous or sedimentary rocks beneath Earth's surface become so hot or are squeezed so tightly together that their minerals are changed into new minerals. Metamorphic rock has been born. Its name means "changed in form."

Geologists don't understand just how metamorphic rock is made. Perhaps, when hot magma is pushed up into the bedrock, the solid rock around the magma is "cooked," changing it into metamorphic rock.

This metamorphic rock formation has been twisted by the great pressure and heat that formed it.

This cliff of metamorphic rock was a different kind of rock long ago. It was "cooked" into metamorphic rock by great underground heat and pressure.

Another way this may happen is when deeply buried rock shifts about and is squeezed tightly together. This great pressure could change the rock into metamorphic rock.

Later, the new rock may be thrust up as a mountain range. Layers of this changed rock often are twisted and folded into the shape of ocean waves.

One example of metamorphic rock is the black and smooth *slate* of your classroom chalkboard. Another example is the rock type called *marble*. Marble is limestone that has been changed into a metamorphic rock.

The metamorphic rock marble was once soft limestone that was turned into marble by heat and pressure deep underground. Sculptors like it because it is easy to cut and polish.

31

THE ROCK CYCLE

All through Earth's history as a planet, its rocks have been changing. Deep within the rocky crust, heat and pressure change older rock into new rock types. Volcanoes pour out magma that hardens into rock. And all the while at Earth's surface old rocks are chipped, broken, and worn away by *weathering*. This never-ending breakdown of old rock and the forming of new rock is called the *rock cycle*.

The effects of weathering can be seen here. Rain and blowing sand over thousands of years eroded and smoothed this granite rock formation on Kangaroo Island, Australia.

The rock cycle started when Earth first formed as a planet. The cycle goes on to this day and will keep going on for billions of years to come. The rock cycle is endless and accounts for all the rocks that we see everywhere. Let's follow the several paths of the rock cycle by working our way through the diagram on page 36.

 Erosion by water often cuts away and exposes the soil beneath the ground cover. The soil may then be washed out to sea where it will be compressed to become sedimentary rock. Erosion, or weathering, is an important part of the rock cycle.

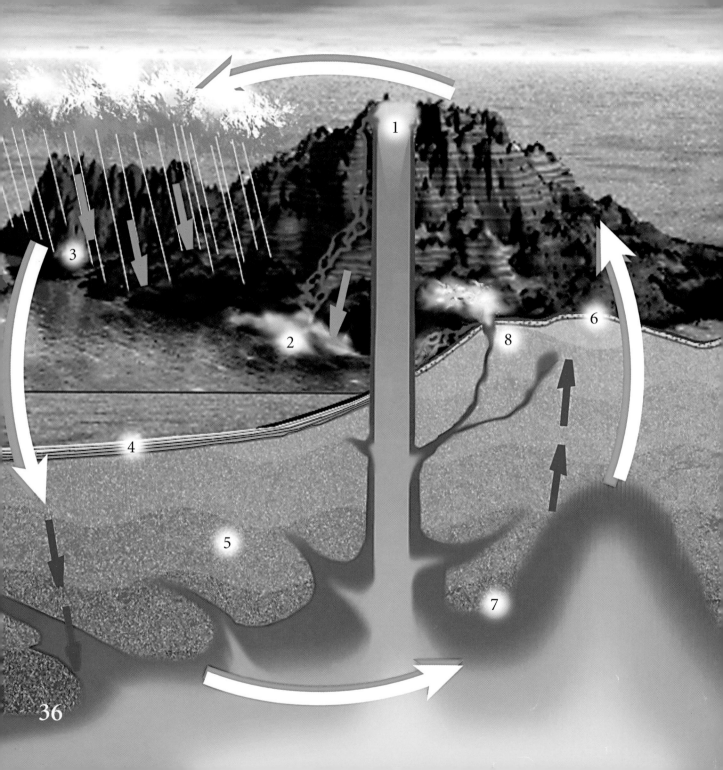

1. Starting at the top, the hot magma wells up from deep inside the planet to the surface. It cools and hardens as igneous rock. Two things can then happen to the igneous rock: 2. If it gets covered over and pushed deep underground, it will be heated and crushed to become metamorphic rock; or 3. it may be worn away by weathering over thousands of years and turn into sediments. 4. Layered on the seafloor, the sediments are packed and cemented into sedimentary rock. 5. If the sedimentary rock stays deep within the seafloor, it eventually is heated and pressed, becoming metamorphic rock. 6. If thrust up to the surface, the metamorphic rock is then broken down by weathering and crumbled as sediment. 7. Or, if the metamorphic rock remains deep beneath the seafloor, it melts and is changed into magma; 8. The melted metamorphic rock may be pushed up to the surface as magma and harden into igneous rock.

HOW ROCKS ARE USED

What would our world be like without rocks? Think about this: limestone and clay are crushed to a fine powder and mixed with water to make cement. What would your town be like without cement?

Stone figures carved out of lava have stood erect on Easter Island in the southern Pacific for centuries. They remain a mystery. People have long made such stone carvings to honor their gods and heroes.

Rocks are used in many other ways. Marble is easy to cut, shape, and polish. It is used to make statues and the walls and floors of elegant houses and museums. Crushed rock chips are used for driveways. Granite is cut and polished and used for gravestones. The great cathedrals and castles of old were hewn from stone. For about seven thousand years, clay has been used to make bricks in many parts of the world. Clay is also used to make pottery, tiles, and fine porcelain figures.

Yes, a world without rocks would be an empty one indeed.

Thousands of cathedrals, castles, and huge monuments, such as this medieval tower in Italy, are reminders of the many ways people have used stone throughout the ages.

DID YOU KNOW?

- The oldest rocks found on Earth are about 4.3 billion years old.

- The oldest known rocks are *meteorites*. They are about 4.6 billion years old. They mark the time when Earth and the other planets were formed.

- The beautiful rock formations—stalagmites and stalactites—in limestone caves are formed by water rich in minerals dripping off the cave ceiling and solidifying over hundreds of years.

- Rocks were among the first weapons and tools used by people more than a million years ago.

- A tiny grain of sand (a rock) inside an oyster causes the oyster to coat it with calcium, which eventually becomes a pearl.

- Silicon, which sand is made of, is used in computer chips. Ever heard of Silicon Valley in California?

Meteorites—pieces of rock and metal from space—are the oldest known objects reaching Earth from space. This nickel-iron meteorite is from eastern Russia and fell in 1947.

GLOSSARY

Basalt   An igneous rock that has hardened from the molten rock magma. Basalt has very small grains.

Bedrock   The solid sheet of rock that forms Earth's crust. Sometimes it is exposed, other times it is covered over by soil.

Conglomerate   A rock made of rounded pieces of other rocks cemented together by mineral "glue."

Fossil   The remains or imprints of animals or plants preserved in rock and older than 10,000 years.

Granite   An igneous rock that has hardened from the molten rock magma. Granite has large grains.

Igneous   A word meaning "fire" and the name of any kind of rock that hardens from the molten rock magma, such as basalt and granite.

Lava   An igneous rock formed from the molten rock that pours out of volcanoes.

Limestone   A soft sedimentary rock formed from the skeletons of clams, snails, and other sea animals.

Magma   The molten rock beneath Earth's crustal rock. From time to time magma wells up through cracks in Earth's crust or up through volcanic vents.

Marble   A type of metamorphic rock often polished and used to decorate buildings.

Metamorphic   A type of rock that has been changed into a still different rock type by heat and pressure deep underground.

Meteorite   A small piece of rock or metal that has reached Earth from space.

Mineral   Any element (such as gold) or compound (such as quartz) found in nature and that has an orderly and fixed pattern of its atoms.

Obsidian   An igneous rock formed from magma that cools very quickly and turns into volcanic glass.

Rock cycle   The never-ending process of rock formation.

Sandstone   A sedimentary rock type made of sand.

Slate   A type of fine grained metamorphic rock. Once used for chalkboards.

Sedimentary   Any rock type that is made up of sediments.

Sediments   Earth materials including clay, lime, sand, gravel, and sometimes plant or animal remains.

Shale   A sedimentary rock type made up of mud and silt.

Weathering   The wearing away of Earth's surface by the action of wind, water, and other elements.

FIND OUT MORE

Books:

Bass, Lin. *Rocks.* NY: Golden Books Family Entertainment, 1991.

Bell, Robert. *Volcanic Rocks.* Science Up Close series. NY: Golden Books Family Entertainment, 1994.

Challoner, Jack. *Learn About Rocks and Minerals.* Learn About series. NY: Lorenz Books, 1998.

Downs, Sarah. *Earth's Hidden Treasures.* NH: Twenty-First Century Books, 1999.

Horenstein, Sidney. *Rocks Tell Stories.* Beyond Museum Walls series. CT: Millbrook Press, 1996.

Morris, Neil. *Rocks and Minerals.* Hotshots series. Crabtree Publishing Company, 1998.

Oldershaw, Cally. *3-D Eyewitness: Rocks and Minerals.* NY: DK Publishing, 1999.

Packard, Mary. *Rocks and Minerals.* NJ: Troll Communications, 1997.

Pinet, Michelle. *Be Your Own Rock and Mineral Expert.* NY: Sterling Publishing, 1997.

Websites:

National Museum of Natural History (Smithsonian):
http://nmnhgoph.si.edu/

Athena, Earth, and Space Science for K-12:
http://inspire.ospi.wednet.edu:8001/

Learning Web at U.S. Geological Survey:
usgs.gov/education/

Cape Cod Rocks:
http://www.capecodrocks.com

The Discovery Channel School:
http://school.discovery.com/

Volcano World:
http://volcano.und.nodak.edu

Ecokids:
http://ecokids.earthday.ca

Let's Find Out About (general science):
http://letsfindout.com

Pop Magazine (science for kids):
www.popmagazine.com

AUTHOR'S BIO

Roy A. Gallant, called "one of the deans of American science writers for children" by *School Library Journal*, is the author of more than eighty books on scientific subjects. Since 1979, he has been director of the Southworth Planetarium at the University of Southern Maine, where he holds an adjunct full professorship. He lives in Rangeley, Maine.

INDEX

Page numbers for illustrations are in boldface.